Correspondent

Correspondent

DOMINIQUE BERNIER-CORMIER

icehouse poetry
an imprint of Goose Lane Editions

Edited by Anne Michaels.
Cover and page design by Julie Scriver.
Cover illustration: Pexels.com.
Printed in Canada.
10 9 8 7 6 5 4 3 2 1

Library and Archives Canada Cataloguing in Publication

Bernier-Cormier, Dominique, 1991-, author
        Correspondent / Dominique Bernier-Cormier.

Poems.
ISBN 978-1-77310-013-5 (softcover)

        I. Title.

PS8603.E76195C67 2018   C811'.6   C2018-901165-3

We acknowledge the generous support of the Government of Canada, the Canada Council for the Arts, and the Government of New Brunswick.

Goose Lane Editions
500 Beaverbrook Court, Suite 330
Fredericton, New Brunswick
CANADA E3B 5X4
www.gooselane.com

pour mes parents

The world cannot be translated.
It can only be dreamed of and touched.

Dejan Stojanović, "The World II"

Il y a dans le regard du désordre cette hirondelle de menthe et de genêt qui fond pour toujours renaître dans le raz-de-marée de ta lumière.

Aimé Césaire, *Cahier d'un retour au pays natal*

Prologue: *I Feel So Strange Writing*

I feel so strange writing

Je me souviens de tout de la bouche pleine d'or de Marina

to you in this language we never speak Papa

les grues qui hissaient un soleil rouge hors du brouillard

with words I didn't own when all this happened

chaque matin les murs du Kremlin le long de la rivière

do you remember the sound of English before meaning

à Izmailovo la fumée bleue des shashliks les clins d'oeils métalliques

I remember English as a river flowing from the radio

les marchands de kvass le pain noir en bouteille

and now all these words like ice cubes in my hands

le khachapuri au café Georgien les petites tables rondes

threatening to melt into noises again I feel so strange

les gaïs dans leurs manteaux gris acier le bois poli des Kalashnikovs

writing but I try to remember that all poetry is translation

le lac vert du gazon de l'ambassade américaine

and that translation is not betrayal Papa

aux portes les Marines qui glissaient leurs miroirs sous notre voiture why does the language of my dreams feel so political

        les grands poumons de cristal accrochés au plafond du métro

to translate as in to carry across the sea

        les balles de tennis brilliant dans le crépuscule bleu de Luzhniki

how often our bodies were translated across borders

        la grande voix rouge de Micha Молодец! Молодец! Молодец!

so many are not allowed to cross

        les fenêtres en feu de l'Hôtel Ukraine le soir, du balcon

how lucky to simply leave one tongue behind Papa

        chaque matin l'énorme oignon doré de Saint-Sauveur

when it hurts to speak it and more than anything

        mes doigts sur le piano parlant mieux le Russe que ma bouche

I hope you taught me well and I don't drown

        dérouler les longues pages des boulots blancs à la dacha

these other voices with mine I hope

        se jeter dans la neige comme dans un lac calme

I remember it is the correspondent who is foreign

        la belle voix argentée de Galina de l'autre côté d'une porte

not the landscape

        la lumière de Moscou et son fantôme dans ma gorge

KURSK

It takes great courage to speak in fragments.
It takes great courage to speak in whole sentences.

Mary Ruefle, "On Secrets"

During a naval exercise on the morning of August 12, 2000, Russian Oscar II-class submarine Kursk sank to the bottom of the Barents Sea within minutes. One of its badly maintained torpedoes had exploded in its launching tube.

The Russian Navy did not realize the vessel had sunk for more than six hours, and took over sixteen hours to locate it. Russian officials then misled the public regarding the cause of the accident and the progress of the rescue mission, announcing that communication had been established with survivors trapped in the submarine.

Meanwhile, newly elected President Putin refused all offers of help from foreign governments despite Russia's own rescue submarines being unavailable, having been loaned away to a private company gathering artifacts from the Titanic wreck.

At the time of the sinking, my family had been preparing to move from Quebec City to Moscow, where my father had recently been named Foreign Correspondent for CBC/Radio-Canada. He left ahead of schedule to cover the sinking and rescue of the Kursk, and we followed him at the end of August.

Eighteen years later, the families of deceased Kursk sailors are still fighting for government transparency and accountability for the loss of their loved ones.

A red bulb drips from a ceiling of steel. Dmitry reaches for a pencil in the pocket of his ironed shirt. He tests the sharp tip of lead, traces a line in his palm. Oxygen drains from the thick air. Like breathing in bricks. A church at night, full of smoke. Dmitry flattens the wrinkles out of a loose sheet. Water leaks onto the paper from the escape hatch, a chandelier of seawater. His wrist moves in the dark. His name: *Lieutenant-Captain Dmitry Kolesnikov.* The time and date: *13:15, August 12, 2000.* Pins and needles in his arm from breathing in carbon monoxide. Like being tattooed by air itself. Still, his Russian flows in calm waves, steady strokes. The zeros floating above the line like hopeful silver bubbles.

It's 13:15.

At our seaside cottage in New Brunswick, our mother teaches us difficult strokes: butterfly, Cyrillic. My palms learn new ways to hold pens and waves. I point Moscow out to my brother on a deflated beach globe. I already know the words *water, broken,* and *why.* I write pages and pages of

м м м м м м м м

waves that never crash, frozen. We storm the beach waving sharp sticks, pretend to be Napoleon's soldiers crossing the Moskva. I wear a dead jellyfish as a crown, a cape of algae. Behind a bay window, my mother packs boxes, wraps glasses in thousands of little bubbles. She writes *books, fragile, personal* in black marker in a language she can't read yet.

All personnel from sections six, seven, and eight have moved to section nine.

My father sits on a flowered couch in St. Petersburg, a notebook open in his lap. Irina Kolesnikova slides her son's wedding tape into the TV's mouth. From the corner of his eye, my father can see Dmitry's empty room. Dumbbells rusting on the floor, little wrecks. On the TV screen, a dove bursts from cupped palms. They watch in silence until the tape clicks to black. Roman Kolesnikov brings out a silver tray with glasses and a bottle of cognac. Tania, my father's interpreter, translates three toasts. The Kolesnikovs hold a photo of their son for the camera, their hands shaking. Outside, young men with shaved heads snap branches of silver fir. They brush the snow off a bronze plaque, pass a flask around. Before each swig, they read his name aloud.

There are 23 of us here.

Early morning, August 12. Hydrogen peroxide leaks from an I-15 torpedo aboard the *Kursk*. Liquid falls, drop by drop, onto a ring of copper insulation. At 11:29 a.m., seismographs in Norway detect an event of magnitude 1.5 on the Richter scale. The submarine sinks 108 metres to the bottom of the Barents Sea, fire in its hull. Two minutes later, a second torpedo explodes in its launching tube, triggering a chain reaction. Torpedo heads burst one by one, a long rosary of flames. Seismic needles shake as far as the New Mexico desert. Scientists in white coats and round glasses analyze scribbles of lead, pinpoint the location of the event fifty miles off the coast of Kola, in Russia. Holes in the hull the size of bodies. The whole sea trying to squeeze itself in.

We feel bad, weakened by carbon monoxide.

My mother, at fourteen, swims for hours before school every day. Her palms cup water, wrapped in bracelets of silver bubbles, rosaries of air. She breathes to the rhythm of morning prayer. *Je vous salue Marie, pleine de grâce.* A kick on *Marie,* a breath on *grâce.* Clockwork. Outside, nuns circle the pool in their black habits. Hands behind their backs, the white clouds of their voices. Snow falling on Quebec City's copper roofs. A bell ringing. When she swims the backstroke, my mother balances a cold glass of water on her forehead. To learn to keep still. To learn not to shake when she runs out of breath, when breath runs out of her. The glass throws a ring of light across her freckled face. If it falls into the water, the clock will stop, go back to zero.

Pressure is increasing in the compartment.

At a mansion on the Black Sea, journalists snap photos of President Putin lifting weights, grilling meat over a fire. At the banya, women slap his naked back with branches of birch. To improve circulation, blood flow. A bodyguard stands in the steam room in a black suit. The president's face plugs the hole in the massage table. A clean white sheet covers his lower half. In a room on the other side of the mansion, a telephone rings. An aide runs over with a faxed sheet and a pair of glasses. The president reads it slowly, line by line, then crumples it. He walks outside onto the beach and throws himself in the water, steaming. A white fist of paper floats up, breaks the surface. Men in black glasses watch from the shore, whispering into their wrists.

If we head for the surface, we won't survive the compression.

Dmitry can't feel his legs anymore. Sawed in half by freezing water, like a woman he once saw at the circus. Faking a smile, skin full of glitter, sparks. In the dark, the twenty-three men try to stop their brains from counting down. They try to think of sex, light, beer. Seconds pass like years. They punch rescue signals in Morse code against the walls. Short long short. The air thickening like vodka in a freezer. Slow, syrupy. They take turns punching, so the sentence never ends, the wave never breaks. Trying to write on the outside of the ship, their steel fists rising out like Braille. So in a hundred years, tourists will dive to the wreck and run their gloved hands softly along the hull, reading their silent screams.

We won't last more than a day.

Sheremetyevo Airport, August 23, 2000. Every sign warped, like trying to read underwater. We don't know the word for *exit*, so we follow green arrows until a voice calls my mother's name. Sasha is holding a sign that says *CBC*, waving. He leads us to a muddy Jeep, explaining things with his hands. Through the smog, I see cranes moving in fields like great animals. A red sun shines through the freckled windows. I try to read the billboards, but we are moving too fast. The writing slipping like water through my palms. Sasha weaves through traffic over the Moskva. Faces gliding across the grey river. Gold domes growing out of the city. My mother turns, smiles at us. I try to read her face, her neck wrapped in blue flowers. *On est presque arrivé, on est presque à la maison.*

All personnel from sections six, seven, and eight have moved to section nine.

Nadia rises from a sea of black shawls, her whole body shaking. Vice Premier Ilya Klebanov hides behind a bouquet of microphones. *You should shoot yourself now*, she tells him. Her cheeks flashing red. *We won't let you live, bastards.* Every camera pointed at her. Her fist in the air, her mouth overflowing. *You all sit up there bloated, and you left us with nothing, not even a word of hope.* A nurse in civilian clothing breaks from the crowd in the background. She walks towards Nadia, a needle in her hand. A glint of light at the edge of her sleeve. She pushes the last air bubble out, then sinks the needle into Nadia's thigh. Straight to her bloodstream. Nadia unlearns language, unlearns her legs, unlearns grief. The Vice Premier turns his face away as they carry her out the door. The cameras watching her fade.

We have made the decision.

Dmitry pulls the pin on an oxygen candle. The iron powder flares up, lights the faces of the tired sailors for a second. The same cartridges that feed the yellow masks on planes. That keep astronauts alive in their bloated white suits as they float in perfect circles around the earth. The candles suck the carbon dioxide out of the sick air. A sailor's hands shake as he holds one above the rising water, above his head. They take turns, pass them around with both hands so they don't fall into the water. Quiet church. Dmitry imagines the Mir station circling the earth in black space, clicking a photo every second, clocklike. From up there, the worst seas must look calm. The surface still, unbreakable.

because none of us can escape.

Sasha's hands steady on the wheel, merging onto the Moscow Ring Road. He teaches my mother new words. *Paper. Sorry. Fall.* Freezing his mouth into an *O* so she can mimic it. A crowd of stuttering exhaust pipes. In the backseat, we make faces. Stare at the stars of the Kremlin towers glowing red in the dark. A *gaï* blows his whistle, points at us. Striped uniform. Blue. Fur. Gun. Our licence plate screams foreigner. 003: Canada. K: correspondent. *Papers, please.* Sasha grabs a few loose sheets from the glove compartment. The *gaï* leans his Kalashnikov against the window. The black muzzle a little eclipse against my cheek. My mother turns around, freezes. Her voice doesn't shake. *Ils font juste nous dire bienvenue, mon chou.* A fist reaches back in, full of paper. He waves us off.

It's dark here to write, but I'll try by feel.

Nadia Tylik welcomes my father into her home in Alapa, on the shores of the Black Sea. In a corner of the living room, a shrine to her son. A photo of Sergei playing on the beach as a child. A white pebble in his raised fist. A vial of water filled at the wreck's site, where Nadia threw fresh flowers into the sea. White knuckles on the railing. An idol of St. Nicholas, a gold halo floating above his head. In another corner of the room, a metal cabinet filled with pages of cold words. *Procedural. Alternative. Commission.* My father listens, a microphone wilting in his lap like a black tulip. Tania translates, the taste of grief in her mouth. Outside, waves crash one after the other. My father's pen moves in the margins:

why why why why why why why why why

It seems there are no chances,

Yuri Gagarin's steel eyes look down at us from the sky. His face a tower. His metal arms shooting straight from his body like sharp wings. In his hand, a helmet the size of Sputnik. We pull up to the gates: *Star City.* We buy tickets and are led through hallways to a wide window. Behind it, men and women type green letters on black screens, their backs turned to us. Bulbs light up one by one on a wall, drawing a flight path. We are led through hallways to a swimming pool. At the bottom of the clear waters, the wreck of a space station. Bodies moving through flooded doorways in slow motion. Through water, hands appearing to shake. Disappearing into hatches, holes. A crane pulls a cosmonaut out of the pool, water dripping like pearls from his neck. They land him gently on the ground and take off his helmet. His face breathing, wet.

10-20% at most.

On TV, we watch an underwater camera scan the dark hull. The screen blurry, a wet circle of light, no sound. The anchor freezes the image, draws a red circle around the escape hatch, explains something in Russian. Two black gloves grip the wheel. A diver pounds Morse code on the hull with a tiny hammer, the sounds muted through water. Only a faint, steady clicking. He puts his ear to the metal. Nothing. Searching for strings of air thinner than hair. They pierce the hull with a long, spinning drill, but the airlock is flooded. Dmitry's body floats behind the black door of the TV screen, a note folded neatly in his pocket. Waves of text crash softly down. The only part I can read is a number.

118. Then faces, faces, faces.

Let's hope at least

My father, at fourteen, boards a Russian cargo ship in the port of Saint John, New Brunswick. The captain shakes his hand and pulls him and his friend on board for a tour, tourists in their own home. A strange country of steel floating in familiar waters. The hold bursting with sacks of gold wheat. My father and the captain talk in broken English, talk in circles. Russian men look up from their meals, spoons frozen in air. They wave hello. The captain points at valves and dials, saying words in Russian. A needle points to *rain* on the face of a barometer. The captain knocks on the metal wall, says *strong*, rolling the *R*. Back on the open deck, he hands my father a blue and white grammar book. On the drive home, it lies closed in his lap. He runs his hand over the rough cover, imagines the secrets trapped inside.

someone will read this.

Dmitry's wife Olga charges two hundred dollars for an interview. One hundred more for a copy of the wedding tape. News stations loop a video of her visiting the *Kursk* with Dmitry. Olga bending through round doors, smiling at the camera. Dmitry giving a thumbs up. There is a sauna and even a swimming pool on board. They hold up their hands to show off two gold rings around their fingers. At the funeral, my father spots Olga through the church window, head bent. A priest sinks a silver cross in water, raises a fist wrapped in a prayer rope above her. His lips moving in silence. Hot light drips on her fists from a candle she carries with both hands. Outside, cameras roll in the rain, waiting for the doors to open, for the black flow of bodies.

Here's the list of personnel

Divers wrap a long diamond-studded chain around the hull. Slowly, it saws the nose off the submarine. A barge named *Giant* drops steel hooks 108 metres to the bottom of the sea, attaches them to holes in the hull. Motors roll their *R*'s, roll the long chains back up to the surface. *Giant* pulls the *Kursk* underneath its body like a shadow to the port of Vidyayevo. Cranes lift the rusty wreck out, dripping blond braids of sea. Head on, you can see straight through its empty body. Just a bronze ring floating from hooks in the sky. Where the *Kursk* lay at the bottom of the Barents Sea, divers hammer in a silver cross, lay down a wreath of flowers loaded with lead. With fragments of the hull, the families weld a black bell they ring at dawn every year. A clock crawling along.

from the other sections, who are now in the ninth

Russian class at the *Lycée français de Moscou*. Madame Diot's heels clicking up and down the rows. We shut our mouths, barely breathe. Sharp red bangs, shiny hoop earrings. She raises a fist full of chalk to the blackboard and writes the date. Her wrist moves in beautiful circles. Her red lips freeze into October. My friend Cyril puts an ink cartridge under the leg of his chair and sits. The plastic bursts, sprays ink across the white wall of the classroom. He carves a smiling face into the desk. Madame Diot puts a hand against my throat and asks me to whisper Russia. Slowly. I turn red and my hands shake as I move my fountain pen. Ink flows in foreign waves out of the sharp metal tip. I write my name over and over until my hand cramps, turns into a claw.

and will attempt to get out.

At our cottage, a round submarine clock hangs on the wall. Its hands broken. The time: 11:29. On its face, the word *Kursk* printed in red letters. It was salvaged from the hull when they raised it. My father bought it on the black market. That's the story he tells wide-eyed guests over dinner, after a few glasses. Silence. Waves crashing quietly against the red cliffs outside. Jellyfish floating under their gold halos in the sea. My mother breaks the silence with a smile. The clock is a copy, one of thousands. Russian black humour. She takes it off the wall, puts a key in, and turns with her wrist. The clock starts ticking. She raises a cold glass of vodka, tips it down her throat

without a word.

Regards to everybody.

No need to despair,

Kolesnikov.

MASSOUD

Fear is the cheapest room in the house.

Hafiz, "Your Mother and My Mother"

On September 9, 2001, two al-Qaeda terrorists posing as journalists set up an interview with Ahmad Shah Massoud, leader of the Northern Alliance, Afghanistan's main opposition to the Taliban regime. During the interview, they set off explosives hidden inside their camera and battery-pack belts.

Massoud was, at the time, the most credible national leader for a democratic Afghan government. He had risen to international fame after leading the resistance against the Soviet invasion, driving them out of Afghanistan after a decade of guerilla warfare. After the Taliban had taken power in the 1990s, he and his mujahideen had taken up arms again.

It is widely believed that Osama bin Laden ordered Massoud's assassination in advance of the attacks of 9/11 and the anticipated US military response: without his leadership, the Northern Alliance would be considerably weakened, as would American support on the ground.

Massoud's friend and ambassador to India, Massoud Khalili, was with him during the interview. His passport, which he was carrying in his shirt pocket, blocked much of the shrapnel from the blast.

Massoud was a beloved figure inside and outside of Afghanistan. Tens of thousands travelled to the Panjshir Valley to attend his funeral, and September 9 was later declared a national holiday. He was an avid reader and writer of Persian poetry, and would often recite poems to his soldiers.

On September 25, my father crossed the Tajik-Afghan border into the town of Khoja Bahauddin to report on the assassination and the imminent US military operations.

Massoud sits in a chair by the window, his face angled for better light. His eyes turning from grey to green. He puts a hand on Khalili's shoulder, slips a passport into his breast pocket. *You forgot it last night, my friend.* Khalili thanks him. He pours hot water into two teacups, a watch of steam strapped to his wrist. Across the table, a journalist cleans his reading glasses. He speaks, and Khalili translates his opening questions from English to Dari. Word by word, Massoud's jaw stiffens. The room cools. He watches a cube of sugar darken and vanish in his tea. He picks his cup up from the table, a wet eclipse left on the glass. *It's time,* he says. *You can start filming now.* The cameraman aims the lens at his chest. A click. A red eye opening.

A deafening silence had fallen over the valley.

Outside the Izmailovo flea market, a man spins a black whip above his head, cracks the air open. I flinch, stare. A bear dances, wearing a necklace of steel. Children flip coins over the fence. The bear shakes kopeks out of its fur like drops of water. My mother pulls me by the sleeve. Steam pours from a samovar's silver belly. Rows of matryoshkas disappear over the horizon. I pick one up, split it at the waist. Again and again, until it's too small to have a face. A woman is painting green eyes on a stuffed lion with a tiny brush. Men grill shashliks over flames, wearing blindfolds of blue smoke. They wipe their blades on flowered shawls, wink. Somewhere, a Zippo clicks open and closed, open and closed. Chewing the air in its little silver jaw.

Our house was in chaos.

Dushanbe, Tajikistan. In an old Soviet hotel, my father dreams of Afghanistan. In the lobby, a woman plays a nocturne on a piano. The lid open, a long yawn. Her velvet gown pooling at her feet. At dawn, a rotary phone wakes him. A black Jeep is waiting downstairs. Behind dark windows, a man in a uniform writes him a ticket by hand. An hour later, the doors slide open onto a field, blades of grass flattened by wind. He flashes his passport, a gold spark against the navy sky. Alexei, his cameraman, follows. Childhood nightmares play on a loop in his brain: mujahideen holding blue eyes in their palms, red stars carved into naked backs. Above the helicopter, a thin scythe of moon. No helmets, no clouds. The night shaking. Silver buckles clicking shut, then a lift. A blinding head rush.

My sisters gathered around my mother and wept calmly with her.

Khalili wakes with the ceiling in his eyes. He blinks and his lashes fall off his eyes like ash. His fingernails scattered across the room, flipped off his fingers like coins. To his right, Massoud's body. A dark chest shivering, a mirage on asphalt. His eyelids wet black tulips. His jaw shaved clean by flames. The ceiling fan still spinning, live wires hanging from the blades. A curtain of blue sparks. A teacup full of blood. Khalili tries to speak, but the words boil in his throat —
GodGodGod **I remember how pale**

a slice of white sky across his cheek.
His passport burnt into his chest, hot ink leaking into him like a tattoo. A breeze blowing softly through new holes in his body. The journalist lying next to him,

eyes wide open,   ***her face turned***

split in half at the waist.

That night,

Black blades blur a circle of sky. The helicopter tips its nose, raises clouds of white dust, a bullet through milk. My father moves his jaw, makes his ears pop. On the horizon, mountains like a blue envelope torn open. A red bulb flashes on and off in the cabin. Wind everywhere. My father takes *The Great Game* out of his backpack, tries to read through the turbulence, through his fear:

even the stars could not help   British spies dressed as sultans, secret codes smuggled across borders in turbans. The words shaking in his lap, the wind turning pages with invisible fingers. Suddenly, the helicopter tips over sharp peaks. Green Afghan fields spill under them, the Panj River shining. The sky slows down, stands still. The helicopter's shadow pools across the grass, a pupil growing in a green eye.

From the balcony, I could see

My hands reach for everything.
Kiosks selling war trinkets, copper nothings. Star-shaped medals laid out in neat
rows on velvet sheets. Empty shells strung into necklaces. I wear the big green
eyes of night-vision goggles. I put on a gas mask, grab my neck, pretend to choke
on invisible smoke. My brother leafs through pages of old stamps, old faces. We
walk between mountains of vintage cameras and fox skulls.

my uncle walking around the pool as he cried   Everything drowned
in gold light.

I pick up a small sculpted horse, push on its ruby eye. A blade springs out of
its throat. My mother snatches it out of my hand. She buys a bag of shiny black
cherries, dripping wet. I pop one between my teeth, pull the stem. Spit the red
pit out in my palm like a bullet.

Bodyguards kick

Beyond, I could see   the door open. The room
full of blue heat and moans. The brass knob knocked out of the frame,

a figure   hissing on the floor.

Windows blown to nothing, glass teeth lining the sky. Wet black smoke spilling
fast across the floor. They spot Massoud, kneel around him in a circle. One puts
his palm on his chest, burns it. Another blows the smoke gently off his face. He
opens his eyes for a split second. *Help Khalili first.* They lift him, carry him out
in their arms.

leaning on a wall   Eyes shut and shaking.
His jaw clicking, chewing air. They gently stroke his hair. They put the two
bodies side by side in the helicopter.

their face in their hands.
They place a Qur'an on Massoud's chest.
The gold letters trembling, light on water. Voices singing *Allahu Akbar* in rounds.

A last peak, then flat green fields.

My mother turns on the wipers, cleans leaves off the windshield. I hold a piece of amber to my eye, look out the window. A wasp asleep inside the stone. The whole city turning to beautiful rust. The Moskva curving like a whip. By the side of the road, people build fires under their cold cars. Smoke spilling from the open hoods in white sheets. We drive along the Kremlin wall

My heart   and its horizon of red brick.
I try to imagine the secrets behind them, the dreams behind my brother's soft blue eyelids. Outside our apartment complex, a guard lifts the barrier gate. Tips his cap, blows smoke rings in my direction. My mother turns the key, cuts the engine. The silence wakes my brother up.

could not believe it.

The helicopter touches down in a sandy field. No landing pad, no clean circle to aim for. Mujahideen welcome my father, hands on their hearts. Checkered scarves blowing in the fake wind. Pakhols tipped to the side, always about to fall. In the village, women float by in sky-blue burqas, their eyes eclipsed by lace
Children orbit Alexei,

I still believe   little moons.
They throw the few Russian words they know at him, then scatter into the shadows of an almond orchard. The mujahideen take my father to an office, make him sign his name, lock his passport in a drawer. Outside, Alexei and Tania set up their tent on a patch of grass by the river. The men shake their heads, say

this might be a dream

No, men and women. Cannot sleep together
in the same room. No hotels so they lead them to the only empty building. Planks nailed across the blown windows,

ash streaking up the walls like eyelashes.

and I will one day wake up.

Khalili wakes in teal sheets, his leg in a blank cast. No signatures, no scribbled hearts. Metal screws in his femur to keep it from splitting. In a nightmare, a black camera opens its jaw, swallows him. His eyes barely open. Outside, a German countryside. A lone cow with a bell tied around its neck.

And I will hear   A knock on the door.
                                                                          A news crew walks in, already rolling.
A harsh light. A cameraman changes a light bulb, adjusts a bouquet of violets for a better shot. Khalili starts speaking,
                              rust in his mouth. *I started to open my mouth.*
                              I said 'what' in Persian and the bomb exploded.

Shrapnel like raindrops in the skin of his chest. Doctors popped out the shards with small blades. One by one. Stopped counting after one hundred.

      my father say   *I saw dark blue fire rushing from the camera.*

He holds the last photo of Massoud, taken only hours before the blast, reading a book.
      All the smells and all the sounds went inside of me.

                              "Get up, Ahmad. It is time to pray."

The next morning,

We stand in line in the shadow of Saint Basil's. The domes a bouquet of tulips, petals on fire. Snow melts on the guards' eyelashes and bayonets. I huddle with my brothers. The line shortens. My mother looks above our heads towards the entrance of the mausoleum. A low building of polished marble. I look at my reflection in the façade, my face in a vertical red lake. My mother shushes us, and we step through the door. Inside, everything dark and hushed.

A glass box and something pale in it

we could feel his emptiness   wearing a black suit.
I try to blink the dark away, focus on the shape. Babushkas weep silently around me, their hands reaching across the velvet rope. Towards a face outlined in candlelight, the closed eyes flickering. The lips always about to open. A guard hurries us towards the exit. The white world bursting into my eyes.

Every time I blink,   *in the helicopter.*

his profile flashing in the sky.

I   *Adhan:* to hear, to receive news.
Each dawn, my father wakes to the call to prayer. A voice
                                    longed for him
singing through a megaphone, bent by electricity. He unzips his sleeping bag,
checks his shoes for scorpions. He wanders the village, scribbling in a notebook.
In the fields, children pick the silver envelopes of peanut butter that rain from the
bellies of American planes at night. Behind doors my father can't open, women
lift the blue skies of their veils and tell Tania about their lives. When he says
Massoud's name, his men break
                        to console me   into tears, broken
English. A young soldier agrees to take him to the front. He points, says the
Taliban are sleeping just across the river. He says he knows some of them well,
eyes lowered. His own cousin on the other side. His younger brother.

                        Back in his room in the evening, my father flips
open his satellite phone. The green keys lighting his face. He imagines my mother
throwing open the blinds of their bedroom,
                                    cold Russian light
pinned in her hair. Bad reception,
                        through the turbulence
                                    her voice shaking in his palm.

1988, Panjshir Valley. Sediqa waits for her husband at home, the sky sliced open every night. The silver scissors of Soviet planes. Little kicks from inside of her. Massoud riding across a high pass somewhere, his horse halved in snow. She looks out the window, imagines him making his slow way towards her across the Hindu Kush. Inside the mountains, emeralds glowing in the dark like eyes, unseen.

I imagined I lay in a soft field of grass   A long chain of hands passing a scrap of paper with the name of their unborn son on it. A few drops of ink in a pocket spelling *Ahmad*. When the sky boils over, she runs to the river. Hiding from the blond men in their planes, a shield of water. Little kicks in the river.

Quiet.   *and closed my eyes.*

In the next valley, flaming apricots hang from branches at night. Little kicks in the dark, little sparks. A child learns by heart the lines a tank writes in the wet grass.

Across the street, a red sun sets the windows of Hotel Ukraina on fire. The tallest of Stalin's seven sisters. We huddle on the couch in our pyjamas. My mother holding a remote in her lap. Static sky, bad reception. The TV clearing its throat. My father's body, cut in half, moving up and down the screen. A news anchor says his name and his face appears. We cheer, scream *Papa!* Behind him, children climb in and out of the shell of a rusty tank, wave at the camera. My father's face and arms darker already, his mouth speaking

The whispers of

water   a foreign language.

He is looking straight through the camera, into our living room.

My mother's eyes.   consoled me.

We ask her to translate, but she is far away. Her eyelashes combing the sky for silver slivers. Her mouth a door left open in winter.

Jet-lagged, my father wanders the house, finds himself outside the room. He puts his green eye against a slit between the planks. The blast froze the room like a photograph, a dark flash of ash. A quick eclipse, leaving bright shadows on the floor.

Everything a negative of itself.

An armchair tipped over, a hole in its back. A fan hanging by a thread, its blades quiet. The camera gutted on the floor. My father tries to picture it. The click, the red eye of the camera.

They opened   The journalists opening up,

the blue fire rushing into Khalili's mouth. He turns away, his iris cooling as he walks back to his room. He imagines Massoud walking through

the same doors,   *a metal door*

the same light through the same windows
hitting his face. He whispers to his ghost in French, asks him if he saw it coming, a shadow at the corner of his eye. No answer, just wind. He lies back in his sleeping bag, takes out a photo of us. The click of the flashlight, then our faces in his hand.

Overexposed, missed.

From their garden, Sediqa watches the valley flood with bodies,

and brought out　　　a white sliver
　　　　　　　　　　　　pulled from a helicopter. Her daughters
crying in a circle around her, cold glasses of milk to soothe their throats. In
the distance, Ahmad sits on the tank that carries his father's body. Thirteen,
armoured in blossoms. The coffin wrapped in a green, black, and white flag. Men
pounding their chests, Massoud's face in every raised hand.

Ahmad's face
　　　　　　　a white object,　　　the only calm one. He walks up to a stage,
a microphone in his fist. Sediqa watches, imagines a black tulip raised to his lips.

I want to follow in my father's footsteps.
His voice in her ears, ringing. Grief

　　　　　　　　　　　　　　　　splitting her at the waist.

That winter, the market burns down. On TV, smoke rises out of windows like black flowered shawls. A man packs up his matryoshkas, a crowd pushed back into one body. Ten thousand acres of burning, handwoven rugs. Blue porcelain cracking in the heat. Flames peeling the gold onion domes.

something I didn't know   Black ash falling, the sky a static screen. The next day, we drive by to see what's left.   *on the earth*
A babushka walks through the rubble, picking up the green marble eyes of lions turned to clouds. Firemen in white T-shirts spray water into the sky. They sing love songs, steam rising off their shoulders. Tears in their eyes from the heat. Coins melt at their feet, shining like lakes seen from a plane at sunrise. I think of the chained bear, imagine him jumping through a ring of

fire, escaping.

Sediqa hears his voice in the garden, calling her name. She goes to the window. *Too much fog to take off. I'll leave tomorrow. Bring the camera down, I want to film you.* On the terrace, he takes the camera from her cupped palms. A silver bird, one wing flipped open. He asks her to sit on the swing, puts the scope to his eye. She smiles, turns her face towards the valley. A soft focus of fog. The children run out of the house, screaming his name. They take turns filming, being filmed.

I walked towards   Fatima. Mariam. Aicha. Nasrine. Zora. Ahmad.

That night, she wakes up to his face above hers. *Pari. Don't sleep yet.* He takes her by the hand through the garden. Nightgown, bare feet. He whispers ghazals to her as they walk, their fate glowing softly in the lines. She explains the future of the garden. Which tulips, which shadows she wants to plant. He looks up. *We will never see this moon again.* Dawn gathering in her uncovered hair

the white cloth   like milk in black tea.

I gently lifted

Under my sheets, the door cracked open. A thin blade of light. My brother sleeping above me. I count his breaths, listen for a key in a lock. My mother's hushed voice. Outside the window, trees blink their endless red eyelids. In my dreams, the ceiling fan turns into a whip. I turn into a bear. Gold coins rain from black clouds. I wake up to a voice whispering my name, lifting the sheet from my face. My father's face floats above mine, dark and smiling. I throw my arms around his sunburnt throat and he laughs. He turns on the bedside lamp, a hole of light. He sings a French song, waits till I fall back asleep. His hand on my slowing chest. In the morning, he sits at the kitchen table, flipping through a book of Hafiz, blindly.

The words like   *the cloth*   of words in water: unreadable.
                      reflections

and saw

my father, Ahmad Shah Massoud.

NORD-OST

Do you still think the world is vast? That if there is a conflagration in one place it does not have a bearing on another, and that you can sit out in peace on your veranda admiring your absurd petunias?

Anna Politkovskaya

In the evening of October 23, 2002, a group of armed Chechens rushed the stage during a performance of the musical Nord-Ost *at Moscow's Dubrovka Theatre, taking more than eight hundred audience members hostage and demanding the immediate removal of all Russian forces from Chechnya.*

Negotiations between the Chechens and Russian officials lasted three days, but did not lead to a resolution. At dawn on the fourth day, Spetsnaz Special Forces pumped an unknown chemical agent through the ventilation system, then raided the theatre.

All of the Chechen terrorists were shot dead, and more than 130 hostages died from the poisonous gas. Russian officials did not disclose the identity of the gas to hospitals and did not warn them about the attack. To this day, the Russian government has not released additional information about the chemical compound, and families of the victims continue to demand a criminal investigation into the matter.

In the months following the attack, President Putin increased large-scale military operations against Chechen separatists, and the Russian government approved a broad array of new anti-terrorism laws, including restrictions on media coverage of terrorism.

Victor, my brother's nine-year-old classmate, and his mother, Natasha, were in the audience when the Chechens took the theatre hostage. Movsar Barayev, their leader, demanded that all Muslims and foreigners immediately make themselves known. Natasha, who held French citizenship, grabbed her son and two other Russian children sitting close by and walked towards the stage.

When we fly back to Moscow each fall, we can't sleep. The words *jet lag* shiver down our spines. We delay bedtime, take endless hot baths. Try to steam ourselves to sleep. I lie awake in bed, conjugating the verb *sleep* in Russian.

I remember so well   I pick the declensions of *flower* like petals off a flower. I count backwards, my head a microwave full of glowing green numbers. I get up, sneak into my parents' bedroom. I shake my mother's silk shoulder. She sits cross-legged with me on the kitchen tiles, teaches me to slow my breathing. Like her, like a swimmer. She lifts the fear from my chest like a blind. We look at the Moscow night together, whisper. The street lights just holes through which tomorrow already shines.

She tells me to mime the ocean with my lungs, the night
these women's faces   with my eyes.

Outside the Lycée, my mother breaks the circle of fur. She says, *Bonjour, les filles!* Her Quebec accent rippling in the polished lake of their French. Natasha is telling everyone about a new musical. A woman says it's the talk of the town. All the rage. Worth the money, worth taking the pearls out. The glory of the Russian Navy. Golden year, 1913. Doomed lovers, letters lost at sea. And the voices. The voices.

I'll never see faces like that again My mother says she has tickets for the whole family next week, she's heard it's a packed house every night. A bell rings. They flick their cigarettes, the embers little red eyes blinking in the snow. Doors burst open. We come running, screaming down the steps. My mother looks for us, picks our voices out

and the look in their eyes like sea glass in the sea.

Natasha leads Victor by the hand across the street. They climb the marble steps towards the theatre. Across the façade, a sky-blue banner, painted rays of sun. Letters the size of bodies. Hopₐ-Ocт. In the lobby, two women in black blazers chew gum behind a counter. Natasha drops a coin in a glass jar, hands them their coats. Behind, a room full of fur,

We didn't feel they were   pearls of rain.

A blond usher rips their tickets with a smile. He opens the door, puts a finger to his lips. He leads them in the dark with a penlight. Victor can't tell where his hand ends and his mother's begins. His legs dangle off the seat.

Three knocks. Velvet curtains split open. The conductor raises a baton, a long cigarette about to be ashed. Wind blowing through speakers. Smoke spilling from the wings.

An iceberg of silk.

terrorists.

A neon M hangs like fangs above the mouth of the metro. We step onto the escalator, imagine it's the throat of a Soviet sea monster. So deep we can't see the bottom. I let myself get swallowed, look at the white marble ceiling, the dark veins. Crystal chandeliers shine like teeth. My mother breathes out *magnifique, hiver nucléaire.* Murals of

        They were like us: red-cheeked boys raising their fists into storms. I get split up, caught in a current of arms and shawls, foreign tongues. My mother grabs my hand. *T'es dans les nuages? Tiens ma main.* On the platform, a wind that comes from nowhere, everywhere. The doors opening with the soft sound of curtains. Towards the heart of the city, a man's voice announces the stops. Away from it, a woman's. We sing along to the only Russian song we know:

                        hostages   осторожно, двери закрываются
            They said: *Caution, the doors are closing*

In the wings, actors warm up their voices, paint blue stubble across each other's jaws. Right on time, they step on stage, dance in a long line. Arms locked, smiling. Natasha cleans Victor's glasses on her dress, points. *Regardes, Victor. Comme ils dansent bien, comme ils chantent bien.* Off beat, a man enters stage left. His gun heavier, his stubble darker. The line of dancers breaks. Natasha thinks, *What great actors. Look at the fear on their faces.* The orchestra keeps playing. The man raises his fist in the air, fires. The actors kneel. The conductor's baton freezes in the air. Women in black veils appear in doorways. The man walks slowly to the front of the stage, unfurling a flag.

His voice carrying the salt of the Caspian Sea.

"If we were terrorists, we would have asked for a plane and a million dollars."

A policeman unrolls yellow tape around the theatre. Dogs growl into their leather jaws. Journalists stand in pools of light, shouting into microphones. Cameramen test their zooms on the glass doors, focus on the bullet holes. Men paint their faces the colour of leaves, climb into trees wearing night-vision goggles. They blow smoke rings, eyes glowing green, hanging from the dark branches like unripe fruit. My father tries to find somewhere to stand, the street crowded with sirens and rain. Alexei eases the camera over his shoulder like a sleeping child, starts rolling. Behind him, a boy holds an icon of St. George

What would I have done in their shoes?   slaying a dragon. The slab of wood bigger than his chest. The gold leaves shining like armour in the rain and camera light.

Natasha twists the wedding ring on her finger, runs a hand through Victor's hair. *Shh, shh. Regardes ici, dans mes yeux.* In the voice she saves for lullabies, bedtime stories. Onstage, all the lights turn on at once. The iceberg turns back into silk, the actors' guns into toys. The musicians lower their instruments onto their laps, take their fingers off the holes and strings. Unfill their lungs. Everyone's clear, bright faces breathing fear. Victor looks up at Natasha, opens his mouth.
I, too,

She puts her finger on his lips. *Shh, mon chéri.*

She tries to hold herself together, smile through it. Like through boring small talk, fiddling with the silver cross at her neck. *Yes, yes, how strange. This time of year. And just pouring. How strange.* The man stands in a circle of blue light. No microphone. His voice fills the theatre like cold water.

would have strapped on a belt and gone to blow myself up.

If you are a Muslim or a foreigner, stand up. Come on stage now.

My father walks home from the theatre. He comes in, shakes the rain out of his umbrella. Opening and closing it, the sound of a black wing. My mother turns the TV off, kisses him. They whisper in the hall.

They tried to hide their faces

She takes his coat off, picks the cellphone from his pocket. A street magician stealing rings. We hear his voice, run out of our rooms, jump in his arms. Tell him we were just watching him on TV. My mother leads us to the dining room, a bowl of red beets in one hand. From across the table, she asks my father how he's feeling, turning her eyes from blue to green.

but I saw them weeping .

She asks him if it's safe out there, clicking tongs in Morse code. She drops a beet on my plate like a smoke bomb. Under the cover of steam, she asks him if he needs to go back out tonight. The samovar cuts her off, singing *oui oui oui* at the top of its silver lungs.

Natasha tries to breathe, think. Her brain running towards glowing red exits. Calculating odds, the future splitting into endless branches. She takes a breath, turns to her neighbour and the two girls in her lap. She locks eyes with her, mouths   *They said*

Доверься мне, *Trust me.* The woman nods, hugs her daughters. Natasha grabs their hands, looks at Victor.

"Our brothers have been killed."   *Elles sont tes sœurs maintenant.*
She starts walking down the aisle. Heads turn, eyes follow her. She climbs the steps and stands before the man, the children gathered in her arms. A bouquet of pale faces. He flips through her French passport one page at a time. Stares at her photograph.

ваши дети? *Your children?*   *Our children are dying.*
She nods, refuses to open her mouth, let him hear her voice shake.

Natasha pushes the doors open. She stands in the rain, the red dots of snipers hovering like embers over her black dress. Soldiers rush the children, wrap them in silver blankets. She stands at the top of the glistening steps, rain ripping a mask off her face.

No cafeteria at the Lycée, so we walk the few blocks to the French Embassy for lunch every day. *They handed out juice boxes*

Across the street, Russian teens wait for us in the empty playground. Shaved heads, cigarettes behind their ears. Spinning a rusty carousel, bored. We lower our voices, try to walk by unseen. We whisper so our French doesn't echo in their mouths, distorted. One of them shouts *Napoleon!,* shouts *Fuck you!* He rocks back and forth on a playground horse, wearing a paper hat. They laugh, call us голубой, sky-blue, gay. Victor translates for us, shouts back in Russian. They laugh at his accent, throw pebbles, half-hearted. We run off towards the safe walls of the embassy, half laughing, half scared. We shout *Français! Français!,* out of breath,

and the guards slide the gates open.

and took off their masks.

I saw

An NTV journalist breaks from the line, lifts the police tape. A cameraman and a doctor walk with him. White coat blowing in the wind, wet stethoscope around his neck. Cameras follow them. The city holds its breath. They cross the empty parking lot, hands in the air. A door opens by itself. The lobby dark, quiet. Two men in khakis sit behind a counter, as if selling tickets. A man leads them to an office. Movsar Barayev waits, arms crossed. *You can start filming now.* His long beard shaved clean to blend into the Moscow crowd. *There is a steel ring around Moscow, but we have broken through.* A woman stands beside him, a belt around her waist. Wires like jewellery wrapped around her wrists, neck. The journalist tries not to picture numbers growing smaller and smaller inside her chest.

He points the microphone at her, asks her if she's afraid of   *a grey mist*

death   *coming down.*

At school, we draw Russian ethnic groups from a bowl of papers. I pick Tajik. That night, my father puts a cap on my head, says *tubeteika*. Silver almond leaves woven into black cloth. I type Tajikistan into the computer, print a map, a photo of a mosque by a turquoise lake. The next day, I unroll my poster in front of the class. The mosque peels off, floats to the ground. I recite a few words in Tajik. My *tubeteika* slides off. After lunch, we sit cross-legged in the gym. A woman stands on stage, speaking a language that isn't Russian.

I heard a strange hissing sound,   I hear the word *Chechnya,*

then a row of girls my age dance through the doors. Long red sleeves, gold-laced veils. They spin, faster and faster, boots slicing the air. For a split second every spin, I catch a girl's eyes. Unblinking, proud. The click of her boot, clocklike. I take off my hat, my bad costume. I blush, her eyes so much older than mine.

Hostages stand in line to piss in the orchestra pit. A soprano squats behind a curtain of harp strings. Women in black robes sit scattered among the crowd. *Shahidkas*, Black Widows. The man who wrote the show stands up, walks to the end of his row. He asks if he can sit. The widow looks up, nods. Arabic chants play softly from a radio in her lap. Everything but her eyes covered, a thin banner of sky. They start talking. She is an elementary-school teacher. They talk about Persian poetry, Tolstoy, the beauty of the Caspian Sea. She admits she enjoyed the show, asks him how it ends. She tells him her husband and son were killed by Russian soldiers.

A green field on fire and their laughs. *an empty feeling*

Now only death can unbuckle this belt from her waist. At dawn, she tells him to go back to his seat. She writes a phrase on a scrap of paper,

hands it to him.

like nothing mattered anymore

Recite this at the exact moment of your death, and I will see you again in paradise.

In the parking lot, men burn blueprints into their brains, paint their faces the colour of lobbies at dawn. They slip long tubes into the ventilation system, pump gas through the theatre's veins. Mist rises across the stage, a lake on a cold morning. Hostages hold sleeves over their mouths; a mother hides her son under her skirt. When dawn breaks, invisible men split doors to pieces, fists full of sparks and smoke. Thin red threads cut through the air, tied tight between gun barrels and sleeping foreheads.

soldiers running across the armrests,
Once all the Chechens are dead, medics rush in wearing gas masks. They shine penlights into eyes, wait for an iris to burst open, react. They hold mirrors to mouths, thumbs to necks. Wipe foam from lips with handkerchiefs, load bodies into school buses. A father's hand reaches across the yellow tape. Conducting grief,

an avalanche of snoring, growing   keeping time.

growing growing.

We run through the door, shouting *Galina! Galina!* She is always home, welcoming us. Unlacing her flowered apron, ruffling our hair. Asking us how our day was, correcting our accents after we recite our line: Хорошо, спасибо. Как вы? We walk through the rooms, one by one. No one. I walk into my parents' bedroom. Galina is standing still, her back to us. A pile of clothes on the bed. The TV on mute, the iron frozen mid-air in her hand. Steam pumping from the little holes, the room humid. A fake rain forest. On the screen, wet white sheets in a parking lot. A journalist crying, his face split, half blue, half red. A banner at the bottom of the screen, the Russian script flowing too fast for my eyes. Galina turns around,

        After seeing my son   not seeing us for a moment.
Then she opens her arms, her face breaking into our wet hair.

Words we don't know but understand.

I slipped out of the morgue.

I stopped a car,

Victor walks away from the car. Natasha's hand through the window, still waving long after he turns his back. Her wrist resting on the glass, stilled at a green light. We stand in the schoolyard, waiting for the bell. Victor walks towards us. We gather around, surround him. Little journalists all wanting a piece. He steps onto a bench, clears his throat. His glasses gone. He starts but the bell suddenly rings, drowning his voice. His mouth left open, full of brass.

As we sit down, my father's phone rings in the pocket of his coat. Hanging in the hallway, the light pulsing through dark, wet wool. A stormy sky, rumbling from its little golden hook. He answers it, says his own name. Steps out onto the balcony. His mouth moving behind glass. My mother tells us to eat, that it's

I had no money   nothing.

        so I gave the driver my wedding ring.

Reading his lips, translating the dying light at his back.

On the plane, I look at the emergency sheet. A man smiling as he crawls under smoke, slides a life vest around his daughter's neck,

> jumps into a lifeboat.
>
> ***I jumped off a bridge***

The flight attendant straps on a yellow mask. We fight for the window, wave at the man waving neon sticks. We can see the runway ahead, rows of light showing the plane's future. I imagine the pilot flipping switches. Click, click, then the little fear I love in my chest as we take off. Moscow shrinks to a single light. On the screen, I look at the live map, the red thread we drag across the land. I dream of the plane as a needle, stitching the ocean shut between Russia and Canada. People speaking both French and Russian, at the same time, without words. My brother lifts the eye mask off my face, says *Regardes dehors*.

Below, nothing. No cities,

> ***but I didn't even black out***   just ice breaking quietly.

His voice shook my shoulder

Every hour on the hour, a policeman cracks the door of the hospital to say *niet*. He can't let the families in, he can't give names. Tania makes a phone call, bends the truth. *There's a Canadian hostage. The embassy wants us to check he's alive.* They let her and my father in through the back door. A nurse leads them through hallways, a blue mask over her mouth. Only her eyes showing, crying. She tells them how the paramedics dumped the bodies here, here, here. Threw a handful of syringes, said

shouted in my ear   *Here's the antidote.*

How there wasn't enough, enough beds. Enough of her, her, her. Enough time. How they didn't warn them, kept it all under wraps. The next morning, a doctor tapes a list of names to the glass doors, eyes lowered. The rain falling on families in endless needles.

get out

On the way to the hospital, my mother explains radiation. How waves crash through mémère's body to heal her. My father smuggles in fresh oysters and a little knife in his pocket. He leans over his mother's bed, touches her blue skin. He shucks the oysters, his hands quick and fluent. He lifts a shell to her lips. She smiles, leans back. He touches her chin with a handkerchief. Outside, snow falls into the Atlantic. I watch them through a crack in the door. The green peaks of the monitor, the steady drip.   *get out*

On the car ride back, my father's cellphone rings. He answers, nods, doesn't say a word. He hangs up, gives us the news. The car fills with silence. The only light from the dashboard, needles and numbers glowing in the dark. At the cottage, the waves reach the windows.

I dream of eclipses and submarines.   *get out get out*

In the morning, nothing is like I remember. White, covered, foreign.

I didn't even catch a cold

even though the river was full of ice.

Epilogue: *Dear Ahmad*

Dear Ahmad I don't know you

> *These are the fragments left on the cutting room floor*

and you don't know me but I am writing to you

> *the slow-motion explosions of jellyfish around me in the dark water*

because my father would tell me ghost stories about yours

> *the chaotic milk of a soft September dawn*

and now they have turned into poems Dear Ahmad

> *the first words I learned in Russian peach good-bye embassy*

what a shock to see your profile appear on the screen

> *neon green numbers falling one by one to their knees*

your face a beautiful translation of your father's

> *the phrase a bronze forearm punctured by the rain on a loop in my brain*

your eyes reading these words just a click away Dear Ahmad

> *words galloping furiously at the bottom of a screen*

please believe me I don't claim to know you or your country

> *my mother always the translator of strange hooves*

but I feel strangely close to you our fathers breathing

> *fields and fields of purple eyelids blinking in the wind*

the same air only weeks apart dreaming in different languages

the whistle of a samovar a bowl of pear in the snow

in the same dark room and mine still feeling the heat

a tripod translated into a glowing trident by the blast

that killed yours on his green eyes Dear Ahmad I am not looking

jasmines in an icebox crossing the ocean on a plane at night

for validation no I am not looking for a stamp

in February black clouds like caviar gathered in brass spoons

I know the world cannot be translated but only felt

the red rose of Radio-Canada pinned to his chest

and I have not felt your pain our worlds so far away

the white dome of a mosque peeled like a hard-boiled egg

and yet I feel connected to you somehow the negative

the sparkling suit of a man shot from a cannon at the circus

of a photograph please know I am here writing to you

a glass singing in French as I run my finger around the edge

I am here Dear Ahmad your friend

Massoud's bright face in the corner of an envelope

and foreign correspondent

the blue signature of a mountain scribbled on the horizon

The bold text in *Kursk* is excerpted from two notes written by Lieutenant-Captain Dmitry Kolesnikov in the hours following the sinking of the submarine. The notes were found when the wreck was recovered, and parts of them were released to the media by Vice Admiral Motsak on October 27, 2000. The translation presented here is an amalgamation of those published on the websites of the BBC, the *New York Times*, and the *Guardian*.

The bold text in *Massoud* is excerpted from a public Facebook post written by Massoud's son, Ahmad, on September 8, 2013. The post recounts his experience of the days preceding and following his father's death. The excerpts were edited for syntax and clarity.

The bold text in *Nord-Ost* is excerpted from the documentary *Terror in Moscow* (2003), produced by HBO and directed by Dan Reed, and consists of interview fragments from the following hostages: Irina Kuminova, Lena Baranovskaya, Ilya Lysak, Kristina Koropitian, Ivan Oganesyan, and Irina Fadayeva. These interview fragments were also edited for syntax and clarity.

Notes on the Facts

The historical events around which these poems are centered — the sinking of the *Kursk*, the assassination of Ahmad Shah Massoud, and the hostage crisis at the Dubrovka Theatre — are factual and verifiable, and a matter of public record. I take sole responsibility for any error of fact found in the text.

These events, however public, involve deeply personal suffering for the people involved, as well as their families. I do not take this suffering lightly, and I do not claim it as my own. During this writing process, I have sought to negotiate and reconcile journalistic and poetic impulses — the impulse to report, to witness, and the impulse to imagine, to connect.

I have tried to be as transparent as possible with my intentions and my process. Whenever possible, I reached out to the people involved and their families to let them know about this project and made the manuscript available to them prior to publication. The decision to directly quote Dmitry Kolesnikov, Ahmad Massoud, and the Nord-Ost hostages was made in the hope of amplifying their voices. I hope this book does their powerful words justice.

We all experience public events in private ways; through my father, a CBC/Radio-Canada correspondent who covered these tragedies, my family experienced these three particular events even more personally and emotionally. Their narratives and images became enmeshed with the fabric and rhythms of our everyday lives in Moscow. It is this entanglement that I tried to capture and express here.

At times, during this process, I took some creative license in imagining the sensory experiences of certain characters. Whenever possible, these were based on first-hand accounts.

A portion of my personal proceeds from the sale of this book will be donated to the Massoud Foundation, a non-profit, non-governmental organization established to preserve and spread the values, leadership, and ideals of Ahmad Shah Massoud.

The Massoud Foundation is involved in humanitarian and cultural efforts to improve the living standards of Afghan citizens, increase the literacy rate, and build schools, libraries, and computer labs. It also funds *Mandegar Daily*, an independent newspaper that advocates for democracy, anti-terrorism, and for the elimination of government corruption and inefficiency.

Acknowledgements

Many people supported and made possible the writing and publication of this book. First and foremost, I want to thank my family for their sense of adventure, their openness, and their constant support.

Thank you to everyone at Goose Lane Editions for making this book real, especially David Seymour for guiding me through the process and the icehouse board for believing in this project.

Thank you to Anne Michaels for editing the manuscript and welcoming me to Toronto with open arms.

Thank you to Sheryda Warrener for everything she's taught me, which is everything I know about poetry (except mercurochrome).

Thank you to everyone who trusted me with their work during my time in UBC's Creative Writing MFA program. You continue to inspire me not only with your words, but also with your resilience.

Thank you to everyone in Vancouver. You know who you are, and I wouldn't be where I am without you.

Thank you to Kate for her support, edits, and for going everywhere with me in a Subaru Outback.

I am indebted to the work of countless journalists whose dedication, courage, and eloquence shined a light on these stories.

This book was primarily written on the traditional, ancestral, unceded territory of the Musqueam, Squamish, and Tsleil-Waututh Nations, and the Wolastoqiyik (Maliseet) and Mi'kmaq Peoples. I am grateful to be an uninvited guest on these lands.